DELIVERANCE FROM WITCHCRAFT BIRD

Curses/spell of Witchcraft Birds

"If a bird's nest chance to be before thee in the way in any tree, or on the ground, whether they be young ones, or eggs, and the dam sitting upon the young, or upon the eggs, thou shalt not take the dam with the young" Deut. 22: 6 – 7.

• Bird is a symbol of witchcraft.

• It is the power of witchcraft.

LET US SEE THE BIBLICAL ACCOUNT OF BIRDS FUNCTIONING AS WITCHCRAFT ANIMAL

1.   It functions as abortionist or terminator of good successes and fruitfulness – Ezek. 17:3, *"And say,*

Thus saith the Lord GOD; A great eagle with great wings, longwinged, full of feathers, which had divers colours, came unto Lebanon, and took the highest branch of the cedar:"

2.   It functions as demonic eavesdropper, which go about to divulge your secrets at the Nocturnal Market, in the witchcraft Coven – Eccl. 10:20, ***"Curse not the king, no not in thy thought; and curse not the rich in thy bedchamber: for a bird of the air shall carry the voice, and that which hath wings shall tell the matter"***.

3.   It could also function as **evil planter**. Can plant failure, hatred, sickness, death etc. lots of testimonies confirm this.

4.   The **manipulator of good gifts**

and exchanger of man's destiny.
Ezek. 17:4 ***"He cropped off the top
of his young twigs, and carried it
into a land of traffick; he set it
in a city of merchants"***

5.   It **steals man's wealth** – Deut.
22:7, ***"But thou shalt in any wise
let the dam go, and take the
young to thee; that it may be well
with thee..."***

6.   It causes **premature death**.
According to **Deut.22:7**, you must
act it out in prayers, by command
every strange bird around you to
catch fire and go. Only by this you
can live in good success ***"and that
thou mayest prolong thy days"***

7.   Bird can act as **witchcraft
eyes or mobile monitor.** That
explains why some birds come
around so close to your room, close
enough to pick up all your

conversation. The next you will hear after it devilish crow, is the rumours of your secrets plans, which you only talk about in your room.

8.   It is the landlady of evil tree assigned to **block man's way** – Deut. 22:6.

9.   It can place **embargo on land** and landing properties. Spiritual defilement is carried out by witchcraft bird. When a bird defecates on man's head in the spirit, he becomes abusive odour to all his destiny helpers

THERE ARE TWO GROUPS OF BIRDS MENTIONED IN THE BIBLE:

1. Flying birds / or Firmamental birds or birds of heavens – Gen 1:20
2. Winged bird (which could include tyrannosaur, nocturnal birds,

human bat, flying horse etc.) Gen. 1:21.

The bible intentionally classified birds to these two groups for our better understanding, compare to what we have in the world today.

There are natural birds.

Also the existence of nocturnal or supernatural birds is real.

THE EFFECTS OF THE CURSES TRANSFERRED AROUND BY WITCHCRAFT'S BIRDS

"But wild beasts of the desert shall lie there; and their houses shall be full of doleful creatures; and <u>owls</u> shall dwell there, and <u>satyrs</u> shall dance there. And the wild beasts of the islands shall cry in their desolate houses, and <u>dragons</u> in their pleasant

palaces: and her time is near to come, and her days shall not be prolonged." - Isaiah 13:21-22

1. Transfer of witchcraft spirit and power from generation to generation in a family.

2. The curse of affliction and slavery which compel everyone born into the affected family to be a victim of unconscious bondage.

3. The owls in Africa should not be seen by day, when in some places, if it comes out in evening it portrays a bad omen. Owls are creatures with fetish eyes. God said He will cause them to dwell in or take over Babylonian empire. These witchcraft creatures can only dwell in a family or homes where there is no God or where God has been rejected or homes of people rejected by God. Can that happen? I pray that God

will forbid it from happening to us or anyone around us.

4. Satyrs (Oro in Yoruba) will dance in the house or family, church or company where witchcraft bird curse is. The Bible says, **"And thorns shall come up in her palaces, nettles and brambles in the fortresses thereof: and it shall be an habitation of <u>dragons,</u> and a <u>court for owls</u>. The wild beasts of the desert shall also meet with the wild beasts of the island, and the <u>satyr</u> shall cry to his fellow; the screech owl also shall rest there, and find for herself a place of rest. There shall <u>the great owl</u> make her nest, and lay, and hatch, and gather under her shadow: there shall the <u>vultures</u> also be gathered, everyone with**

her mate" Isaiah 34:13, 14 (various bird and winged creatures mentioned in the verses were underlined by me).

3. A house or person plagued by witchcraft bird shall have no rest, lasting peace, unless Jesus is called in to arrest the situation.

NOTE: Satyr is not a bird but a 'winged bird'. It is the ancient Roman god of sex and fertility. It is a demon with wings. It dances to the tunes of ominous curses and ruins.

Wicked angels and satanic agent can take the form of 'a winged creature' when going for their meeting or when going to attack man in his dream life.

4. Witchcraft curse can only affect sinners. So the witches would not attack you, unless they first try to

entice and to lure you into sin.

5. It causes infertility and bareness

6. It pollutes your Christian prayer life.

7. It causes sudden death and stubborn sickness.

8. (Read Rom 1: 23), they can turn the glory of God in man to witchcraft-bird's meal, once the person commit sin. That is the reason the bible says, sinners are handed over to wretchedness i.e. spiritual suffering

9. It has the effect of turning man against his destiny helpers. It feeds the person appointed to help man in life with demonic chronological report of his family etc. Eccl 10:20 - *Curse not the king, no not in thy thought; and curse not the rich in thy bedchamber: for a bird of the air*

shall carry the voice, **and that which hath wings shall tell the matter.**

SOME BIRDS AND THEIR STRANGE VISITATION

There are some birds, their visit to your life, house, church, company or school can be strangely disastrous. This is strange but it is true.

Let me give you from my over 23 years of experience in ministering deliverance and prayers, some strange birds I have come across and the effects of their visit: based on people's testimonies, experiences and my own experience.

1. **The Owls (monitoring agent)**: their visits result in destabilization, loss of good job, witchcraft sickness

and invitation to demonic meeting.

2. **Vulture (Death arrow):** Its presence carries death messages. It could be for spiritual death, business death, and death of wealth and in most cases physical death. It symbolizes a call for or to witchcraft feast – where witches feed on human flesh and blood.

3. **Bat:** feast of wizard, blood sucking, and keeper of blood bank.

4. **Cockroaches:** Satanic pathfinders, hire killer, and bringer of strange diseases.

5. **Ostriches (family witchcraft):** It sets limitation and determine how far or long its victim stay up. It is the power saying no to uprising in life.

6. **Black bird:** Cruelty, affliction, *frustration*, killing of destiny helpers and collector of annual

donation of blood, life and properties.

7. **Singing Birds/sun birds:** invitation to night initiation. They belong to the monitoring agency or group.

8. **Tyrannosaur birds:** Principalities and powers. They are spiritual glory usurpers. It is a symbol of slavery and override of your rights and privileges.

9. **Strange Eagles**: Spiritual kidnapper. Its presence means your life is in a strong bondage and under intense monitor.

10. **NOTE:** In all these you do not need to be fearful or afraid. You are free from their powers as long as you are born again and can pray. The Bible says, *"And who is he that will harm you, if ye be followers of that which is good?"*

1 peter: 3: 13. The answer is no one.

But, if you are yet to give your life to Jesus, quickly do so now or else, this night will be the longest you have ever had in life.

So, if you really want to decide for Jesus just say these prayers with me.

'Heavenly father of love, I want to thank you for sending Jesus to take my place and die on the cross that I might be freed from witchcraft powers, and the bondage of hell, which I was brought into by my sins. I am deeply sorry and confess that I am a sinner. I have sinned (mention all you have ever done as much as you could remember) and I now repent of them all. I promise to forsake them all, turn to follow you and live for you from today. Forgive me LORD and accept my life. I accept and receive the redemption of my soul provided for by the blood of your only

begotten son – Jesus Christ. Thank you for saving me, in Jesus name I pray Amen.

Wonderful! You are now saved. It is that simple. All you need to do now is to look for a living Church, show yourself to a living Pastor and better still you can contact me for advice on what to do next.

Now, get ready. We are about to challenge the powers of darkness, showering witchcraft curses on your family. All evil trees whispering our names to afflict us through that surname shall dry in the name of Jesus.

Avoid what could lead you into satanic cage henceforth.

WHAT CAN SELL MAN INTO WITCHCRAFT COVEN?

1. **Sin**: stealing and swearing, oath taking or entering into covenant with occult person and by using occult materials, read Zech. 5:1-4.

2. **Polygamy:** when you have witch as step mother.

3. **Star gazers/ enviers**: A Christian must not go to stargazers, palm readers and magicians. It is the acts of the Barbarians. So, if you have been involved in any of these before, you need to be aggressive in your prayer now.

4. **Witch doctor:** if you have visited one before then you need to pray.

5. **God can give man up to be killed by witchcraft birds**. *"Thou shalt fall upon the mountains of Israel, thou, and all thy bands, and the people that is with thee: <u>I will give thee unto the ravenous birds of every</u>*

sort, and to the beasts of the field to be devoured." Ezek. 39:4.

Do not challenge God to battle.

Shalom!

TIME TO SHOUT TO GOD FOR DELIVERANCE

1. Father I thank you for your saving power.

2. Satanic Trinitarian powers dedicated to afflict my father's house, heavy stone from heaven crush them now in Jesus Name.

3. Failure magnifier, your time is up, fall and die.

4. Witches assigned to torment my life in and outside my place of birth, I poison you with the blood of Jesus, begin to fall down and die one after the other till you are consumed.

5. Evil birds whisperings my name in the heavenlies be arrested by fire in Jesus Name.

6. Curses sang on my head by any witchcraft bird shall not prosper. You are removed by the blood of Jesus.

7. Any evil power cursing my head from the coven, I fire back your curses to your head, and I kill you with 'curse – stone' in Jesus' name.

8. Witchcraft symbol in my life catch fire

9. Ancestral embargo placed on my generation break by fire in the name of Jesus.

10. Abortionist of hope, my life is freed from you, release me now and die in Jesus name.

11. Coven terminator assigned to waist my life, marriage, children, labour etc. you are a failure, terminate yourself in the name of Jesus.

12. Demonic eavesdropper divulging my secrets and glory in spirit dark-market, I padlock your eyes and ears with thunder blast in the name of Jesus.

13. Evil farmer planting frustration and fear of death into my life sleep and never wake up again.

14. Abortion of good things in my life, I terminate you today in Jesus' name.

15. Where is the exchange of my infant glory? Appear by fire.

16. I claim back my infant glory from you in Jesus name.

17. Winged powers stealing my wealth, die

18. Witchcraft agents vomiting premature death into my life, die in the name of Jesus.

19. Every satanic bird posted to my house, that one posted to my place of work and my marriage functioning as coven mobile monitoring eyes, I burry the sword of the LORD of Host in your eye; go blind in Jesus' name.

20. Every evil tree from our village keeping the records of names of children born for the village, catch fire, turn to ashes and be blown away by the east wind in the name of Jesus.

21. Evil tree in my Father's compound harboring witchcraft blood bank, be bulldozed by the thunder clap in the name of Jesus.

22. Every tree around the house I live in, sitting witchcraft birds and meeting, I curse you in the name of Jesus, dry now.

23. Flying powers assigned to pollute the heavens above me, fall down and die.

24. Witchcraft mess, coven pollution turning my destiny helper away from me, I stop you and wash you away from my life by the blood of Jesus.

25. Blood sucking bird (Nocturnal bird) visiting my neighborhood at nights, your end has come, drink your own blood and eat your own flesh till you die in Jesus' name.

26. Witchcraft trade fair selling and buying in my father's house scatter by fire.

27. Power trading animal weapon in my family die.

28. Dancing demon beating drum of desolation and sudden death on my matrimonial home, you are a failure, I bind you with chains of fire and drop you into the sea of acid in the name of Jesus.

29. Children killing power, hear the word of the LORD, I and my children given to me by God are for signs and wonders, therefore kill yourself.

30. Coven attack on my bloodline

be terminated

31. Satanic bird sent to give evil sermon on my roof, drop down by the flame of fire and die.

32. I take dominion. I am in charge. I occupy my seat of honour in the name of Jesus.

Shalom!

CONTACT ME: I like to hear from you
With love from The Preacher, Oluyemi Stephen Beloved
Jesus Resurrection Power Dome (aka Christ Advancing Mission Team, Nigeria)
oluyemistef@gmail.com,
www.about.me/thepreacher,
+2348067031214
Follow me on my Facebook Page, My Google+ Community
Check my blog for eBook, Teachings, prayers and deliverance messages at Amazon Store and www.jesusdome.blogspot.com.ng

Donate your widow's mite today to keep us online and to enable us continue to provide free services to people of God in need of deliverance. To contribute please contact us on oluyemistef@gmail.com or via whatsapp +2348067031214. You can send a MoneyGram/Western Union to Oluyemi Stephen Beloved. 21, Adinlewa Street, Akure. Ondo State Nigeria

DELIVERANCE FROM CURSES OF WITCHCRAFT BIRD PART 2

Copyright © September 26th, 2015 by

Oluyemi Stephen Beloved

"More than a dozen died following a day visitation to my Father's house after many years."

*"And changed the glory of the incorruptible God into an image made like to corruptible man, **AND TO BIRDS**, and fourfooted beasts, and creeping things." Romans 1: 23.*

I came from Otan - Ayegbaju in Osun State. The story was told of how my father was killed by his kinsmen.

The story in summary was like this. My grandpa brought in another woman who became stepmother. She was said to be terribly wicked and swallowed some demons whole. She was the challenger in the family line for years. She succeeded in killing anyone who will take position and right of first born male child in the family.

When my father, who was the surviving and the first male child of the family got married; this woman went to warn him never to give birth to male child if he wishes to live. Imagine, after your marriage a stepmother to your husband came in to warn you and your partner not to give birth to a male child and that in the day you do just that, then death is the immediate penalty.

The battle began when I was born as the second child of my father and would be the only male child. He was challenged again by his known family wealth rival – the stepmother. The battle was on for at least four years before she succeeded in killing my father. The woman enjoined many backups from witches who came visiting our *family in form of birds.*

So I was taken away from home after burial, away completely from my father's house. At the time, my mother was heavy with the pregnancy that resulted into our last born. Let me stop here.

STRANGERS IN HIS FATHER'S HOUSE

Years after, my sister was preparing to sit for her WAEC Examination, so I made my first trip home for the first time in many years even before the child who is about to write the West African Examination was born. In our family clan, there are many ancient building. My grandfather's house had become burial ground for many. The next house built by his brother is now in used as family house and that was where we lodge the night I visited home. There is a river within the clan settlement. It has ancient power that I will talk about in another article.

The saying goes thus, no child born into our family abroad/away, on coming home, will enter into the family without bowing down to this river. I went to look at this river, just because I remember I had seen it before in my dreams and as I was turning from the river people had already trooping out from the four building that share boundary with the river. By now they have started talking in twos and in threes and in fours.

Just then I notice big fish are in the river, so I turned back to the river and in order to examine the fish I have to lean on the guarding pipes built around the river. The moment I bent low to lay hold of the pipe, the on looking gossipers roared joyfully and rush to me. They immediately know my name and started to eulogise me without asking for what my names are called.

This pained me once they mention my name and said you are a true son of our ancestral father. What a shame! A deliverance minister! That day I learnt the bitter lesson of ignorance. The truth I didn't know had humiliated me. It is tradition and customary that any stranger visiting my father's house for the first time, if pay obeisance to this river before entering, by this the family will know that he is the true son of the soil. One of the gossipers told me these facts then, I became furious. It is not good to be a stranger in your father's house; either biological father or our heavenly father.

THE WITCHCRAFT BIRDS CAME VISITING PHISICALLY

It was late in the night while listening to mysterious story of things happening in my new world from my little sister, who was living among them. Suddenly, the Holy Spirit opened my eyes and I saw conference of witchcraft birds, gathering outside the building and they entered into each other to form a single body; and are ready to attack. I quickly stop my little sister and burst into speaking in tongues and all of the sudden, loud and strange noises of agonizing birds were heard outside the building, it was close to 11pm. The battle lasted for about 30 minutes. Just before their arrival, following the humiliation my ignorance brought upon me in the afternoon, I have made a careful research into spiritual and traditional backgrounds of the family. So they are too late. I had already gotten understanding and was fully ready for their coming.

The following morning those dancing around me last evening were nowhere to be seen. I went back to my place the following day. More than ten people were reported dead after my departure that day.

Later I was told that witches had attacked my sister and that she was at the verge of death. I again went into second round battle against them and my sister was released when about additional five birds died. For each bird that died, a human that the bird is representing died as well.

WHY ARE THEY AROUND THAT NIGHT?

They came to finish my line off. For years many of them believed I was dead after the death of my father. So my coming that day was a great explosion. You will also remember that wicked step mother's challenge- *'no one will take first son position from my son'*. She left a curse attached to witchcraft bird to trail my lineage. Since I was hidden in the blood of Jesus, it was difficulty for them to locate me until I went to them. I remember one of the women came to me and mention all my names one after the other, she said, she was the first person to carry me when I was taken out of my mother's womb and since that day she had not set his eyes on me again. Then I told her, you will not see me again. She was one of those who died after the death of those strange birds.

NOW TO YOU: WHEN YOU ARE OFTEN BEEN VISITED BY STRANGE BIRDS

Curse of a witch in any family open doors for witchcraft birds and other witchcraft animals to trail those in the family that came with shining destiny or what is regarded as announcing star in the spirit realm.

Note the following:

1. If you are being followed by birds or being monitored daily by birds, it is a strong indication that a witchcraft curse had been laid on your generation.
2. The house where this exists, all the children born into the family with announcing stars shall become an automatic victim. So you need Jesus and must be serious with your prayer life.
3. If your house is been watched by singing birds. It is an indication of throne of wickedness that was once raised in your lineage and was forgotten without closing the covenant associated with it.
4. It means there is a secret that you need to know that you do not know but it is known to the enemy. As long as you are ignorant, the witchcraft birds will continue to prey on your daily human efforts.

5. The witchcraft cobwebs will be used to sow a prison cloth on you and that explain why you are often being preyed upon by invisible cobwebs.

6. The more you pray hard against them the more they reinforce and the fierce the battle become. The first to give up between you and the witchcraft birds will become prisoner of war.

7. The battle was so difficult for you to overcome simply because; you do not have the key to unlock the bowels of secret that go beyond your knowledge.

"What knowest thou, that we know not? What understandest thou, which is not in us? With us are both the grey headed and very aged men, much elder than thy father. Job 15: 9, 10

HOW DO YOU RECEIVE LASTING SOLUTION ON THEM?

1. Maintain a right standing in God. Do away with witchcraft materials.
2. Be ready to fight a long battle. It is not just a daily battle on witchcraft bird no! I am only talking about maintaining your Calvary begotten victory. Once you pray and have evidence of victory, you must maintain that spiritual tempo of vibrancy for long time till all your enemies are dead.
3. Enter sweet fellowship with God. Spend time before God and less time before men
4. Renew your mind-sets and what comes from your mouth Romans 12: 1-2.
5. Stop seeing what the enemy want you to see and stop saying what the enemy want you to say.

Resolve to God only. The Bird will keep coming because they want you to see them as your present problem and to poison your mind-sets to believing that your prayer had not been heard. That is a LIE.

6. Engage in a prophetic and revelatory prayer till you are launch into the deep secrets in your father's house down to the 7th generation.

7. **Locate your destiny prophet**. A carefully and prayerfully chosen deliverance pastor who is in the Lord. You need to go for deliverance under a pastor who had overcome witchcraft bombardments in his father's house.

8. Your life is not in danger just because the enemy says so or you are a victim of curse of a witchcraft bird no! Your life is in grave dangers because you give

attention to witchcraft birds than to your God.

Shalom!

NOW GO TO GOD AND OPEN AN ACCOUNT TODAY

The following prayer points will usher in your needed deliverance. So begin from here...

1. Thank God because you are more than conqueror
2. Any secret that I need to know which is not known to me but is known by the enemies and is being used against me in the witchcraft coven, Holy Spirit exposed it in Jesus name.
3. Throne of wickedness in my father's house catch fire in Jesus name
4. Ancestral mark and incision in my body attracting demonic birds to my house, loose your power in the name of Jesus.
5. Witchcraft birds singing songs of affliction in my environment drop to fire in Jesus name.

6. Hired power against my life and marriage, die in Jesus name.
7. Witchcraft Network operation organized to stop me and frustrate me in life, scatter by fire.
8. The battle that swallowed my father, you will not shake me in the name of Jesus.
9. Witchcraft birds monitoring me around, hear the word of the Lord, you are cursed; fail, drop to fire and die.
10. Champion of my father's house, who had vowed not to see me succeeding in life; die by thunder strike in Jesus name.
11. Ancestral mother tormenting destiny of children in my lineage die in Jesus name
12. Rock of ages! Cleft for me and let me hide myself in you.
13. Fire of Deliverance fall upon my life. Possess me and reside in me.

14. I clothe myself with the blood of Jesus.
15. I am free. The blood of Jesus sets me free.

Note: IF you are blessed with this short prayer eBook, I ask you to do something with it. Review it and advertise it.

Contact me for your personal prayer request on Google Community, my Facebook Page or through Email.

You can also visit me today at Jesus Resurrection Power Dome, Ikere Ekiti. Nigeria.

About The Author

Evangelist **Oluyemi Stephen Beloved** is a sound Teacher of the Word of God. He believes in Team work, he preaches it among the Christian leaders and he practices it. He is a leader by example in all he says acts or does.

He is the founder and the mission Director of Christ Advancing Mission Team aka Jesus Resurrection Power Dome. He has more than two decades of field experience. He preaches mostly about correcting the errors in churches of Christendom as opposing true Christianity.

He is happily married in the Lord.

Printed in Great Britain
by Amazon